D1138654

04245318

What Happens When We Recycle

Metal?

Jillian Powell

W

FRANKLIN WATTS

LONDON • SYDNEY

This edition copyright © Franklin Watts 2014

Franklin Watts
338 Euston Road
London NW1 3BH

Franklin Watts Australia
Level 17/207 Kent Street
Sydney NSW 2000

Editor: Julia Bird
Designer: DR Ink
Art Director: Jonathan Hair

Picture credits: James L Amos/Corbis: 6b, 21, 23.;
Alex Bartel/SPL:13; Myrleen Cate/Alamy: 10;
Vicki Coombs/Ecoscene: 18., 19. Ashley Cooper/Corbis: 11;
Corbis: 15t; Christof Ermel/istockphoto: 6t; Graham Flack/Waste
Watch: 7; Eric Gevaert/Shutterstock: 8; P Glendell/Alamy: 12;
Hein van den Heuvel/zefa/Corbis: 14; James Holmes/SPL: 16;
Imagestock/istockphoto: 22bcl; Kevin King/Ecoscene/Corbis: 24t;
Lo Mak/Redlink/Corbis: 9, 15b; Mediacolor's/Alamy: 17b; Sergio
Pitamitz/zefa/Corbis: 24b; Reuter Raymond/Sygma/Corbis: 25.;
Paul A. Souders/Corbis: 17t; Leah-Anne
Thompson/Shutterstock: 22bl; Mark J. Tweedie/Ecoscene/Corbis:
20; Ewa Walicka/Shutterstock: 22bc; M Willis/Shutterstock: 22br.

A CIP catalogue record for this book
is available from the British Library

ISBN: 978 1 4451 3030 9

Dewey Classification: 363.72'88

Printed in China

Franklin Watts is a division of
Hachette Children's Books,
an Hachette UK company.
www.hachette.co.uk

Contents

About metals

● What are metals?

Metals are strong, long-lasting **materials** that we use in many different ways, such as for building, machinery and packaging.

There are many different types of metal, including **precious** metals like gold.

● Where do metals come from?

Metal is found inside rocks or in the ground. Rocks that have metal in them are called **ores**. Processing metals takes lots of **raw materials** and **energy**.

Aluminium is **mined** from a clay-like material called **bauxite**.

Recyclable

We use metals to make everything from food and drinks cans to fridges, computers, cars, jet planes and bridges. All metals can be **recycled** over and over again and stay just as strong.

Metal packaging comes in all sorts of shapes and sizes.

?

DID YOU KNOW?

Metals can carry both heat and electricity.

Steel and aluminium

Steel and aluminium are the most recycled metals. They are used to make a lot of metal packaging, especially cans. Steel is an **alloy** of iron.

Why recycle metals?

● Household waste

Metals make up about 8% of the contents of the average dustbin. Every year in the UK we use around 13 billion steel cans and 5 billion aluminium cans. Over 10 billion are dumped on **landfill sites**.

● Pollution

When metals are dumped, they don't **rot** away. Metal pollution in rivers, the sea and the countryside is becoming more and more common, where objects like ring-pulls can harm wildlife.

Around 2 million cars are scrapped in the UK each year.

Why recycle?

Recycling reduces the amount of metal waste we throw away. It also saves on the raw materials needed to make new metals.

Saving energy

Making new metals uses lots of energy and creates **carbon gases** that can cause **climate change**. Recycling metals uses up to 95% less energy and cuts the carbon gases given off by 80–95%.

Steel is made in very hot **furnaces**, using coal or electricity.

Collection

● Recycling boxes

Some metals, such as food and drinks cans and aluminium foil, are collected from households in recycling boxes or bins.

GREEN GUIDE

Wash cans and tins ready for recycling. If possible, squash them so that they take up less space in the recycling box or bank.

Metal cans and tins can be collected from home for recycling.

● Recycling banks

You can also take metal to be recycled at metal banks in supermarket car parks.

Aluminium cans in a recycling unit, ready to be recycled.

JUST THE FACTS

- Recycling 1 aluminium can saves enough energy to power a television for 3 hours.
- If we recycled all our aluminium cans we could save 14 million dustbins of waste each year.

Scrap metal

Some scrap dealers collect cars and electrical goods, but these are harder to recycle as they are made from many different materials.

Sorting

Different metals

Metals are sorted into different types for recycling at waste sorting plants. Steel is recycled separately from aluminium. Aluminium cans are lighter and more shiny than steel cans. Labels show which metal they are made from.

A recycling lorry drops off a load of metal cans at the sorting plant.

Magnets

Steel and other **ferrous** metals, such as iron, are attracted to **magnets**. Giant magnets are used to pull out steel cans from other metal waste.

Giant magnets are used to sort steel from other types of metal.

Baling

The steel cans are fed into a machine called a can-densor which flattens them and packs them in **bales** and stacks them on **pallets**. The metal is now ready to be taken to the recycling plant.

Recycling steel

 Steel

Three out of four cans that we buy are made from steel. Steel cans are heavier and stronger than aluminium. They are used to package everything from paint to pet foods, tinned fruit, biscuits and sweets.

DID YOU KNOW? ?

All steel cans contain up to 25% recycled steel.

Steel cans are often called tins because they have a thin coat of tin to keep the contents fresh.

JUST THE FACTS

- Recycling 7 steel cans saves enough energy to power a 60 watt light bulb for 26 hours.
- Recycling 1 tonne of steel produces 80% less carbon gases than making brand new steel.

Bales

Steel cans arrive at the recycling plant in bales. They are shredded and washed in chemicals to remove any tin. Then they are fed with other scrap steel into a steel-making furnace.

The steel is already packed into bales when it arrives at the recycling plant.

The furnace is heated to around 1,700 degrees Celsius.

New steel

Molten iron is added to the steel, and hot air is blown through the furnace. The scrap steel becomes molten and mixes with the iron and **oxygen** to make new steel.

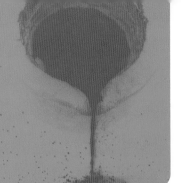

Moulding steel

● Slabs

The molten steel is poured into **moulds**. The moulds are cooled with water to make the steel solid again. When it is hard enough, it is chopped into large blocks or slabs.

The hot molten steel is poured into a mould.

● Sheets

Next, the slabs are rolled into sheets. They can be thin or thick, depending on the type of steel and what it is going to be used for.

?

DID YOU KNOW?

The steel cans recycled each year in the UK save 125,000 tonnes of waste – the weight of 18,000 double-decker buses!

Coils

The recycled steel is rolled into coils and sent to steel-making plants to be made into new products.

Machines wind the red-hot sheets of steel around rollers to make coils.

Can-making

Steel for can-making is coated with a thin layer of tin. It is then sent to the can makers where it is fed into machines that shape it into cans. From here, the cans are sent to factories to be filled and labelled.

At a canning factory, the cans move along a conveyor belt where they are filled by machines.

Aluminium

Conveyor belt

Aluminium is recycled separately from steel. First, aluminium cans arrive in bales at the recycling plant. They are fed onto a **feed conveyor** which carries them into a shredding machine.

The machine shreds the cans into pieces about the size of a 50 pence coin.

Shredding

The machine shreds the cans into small pieces and giant hammers squash them flat. The shreds then go through a strong magnet which removes any bits of waste steel.

De-coating

Next, the aluminium shreds pass into a **de-coating** machine. The machine blows very hot air through them. The hot air burns any paint and **lacquer** from the shreds in about 4 minutes.

The cleaned shreds are now ready to be melted and moulded.

DID YOU KNOW? ?

Some metals can react with foods that contain **acids**, like fruits. Cans are coated with lacquer to protect the food or drinks inside from reacting with the metal.

Waste gases

Waste gases from the de-coating machine go through filters that clean them so the hot air can be recycled. This helps cut down energy use at the plant.

Moulding aluminium

● Heating

The shreds of aluminium are fed into a giant furnace. When the shreds reach melting point, they turn from solid pieces into runny or molten aluminium.

The molten aluminium is poured into a holding furnace before it is moulded.

● Moulding

The molten metal passes into a holding furnace. The holding furnace tilts to pour the molten metal into an upright mould. Samples are taken out to check that the aluminium is pure.

Cooling

Jets of cold water are pumped onto the outside of the mould to cool it. As the molten aluminium cools, it forms a solid shell. The mould is slowly removed. The aluminium now forms a large slab called an **ingot**.

Ingots

The ingots are taken to a mill where they are rolled into sheets of aluminium. These sheets are sent to can makers to make new aluminium cans.

Aluminium ingots waiting to be shipped to factories.

Recycling foil

● Recyclable or not?

Foils are recycled separately from cans. Every year, we use around 35,000 tonnes of aluminium foil for packaging in the UK. It is used for milk bottle tops, baking and ready-meal trays. They can all be recycled. Foils that are coated with other materials, such as plastic, are harder to recycle.

GREEN GUIDE

Use the 'scrunch test' to see if something can be recycled. If it springs back once you have scrunched it, it can't be recycled.

The milk bottle top, kitchen foil and cake holder can all be recycled. The crisp packet cannot.

Melting

The foil is fed with other aluminium scrap into giant furnaces. It is heated and stirred until it melts.

Moulding

Next, the molten aluminium is poured into moulds and cooled. They form ingots which are sent on to **casting** firms. They re-melt the ingots and pour them into casts to make different products, including car parts.

Molten aluminium can be poured into moulds to make casts for ornaments.

New products

Useful material

Many different things, from **aerosols** to ships, can be made using recycled metals.

GREEN GUIDE

Look out for the recycling loop on food and drinks cans. This tells you whether or not they can be recycled.

A steel bridge carries cars over the Panama Canal.

New steel

All steel products today contain recycled steel. They include ship hulls, train tracks, bridges, building materials, household appliances and cans.

Aluminium

Aluminium cans are usually recycled as new cans. They can be recycled in as little as 6 weeks. Foil and other scrap is recycled as different alloys and made into engine and other car parts.

?

Recycled aluminium can be used to make car doors, as well as many other car parts.

What you can do

CASE STUDY

Primary school pupils in Chorley, Cheshire, helped collect aluminium cans for a project to fund fruit trees in Malawi, in Africa. The children grew their own trees in cans for the school grounds and helped to collect cans in recycling boxes and banks. Alupro (the Aluminium Packaging Recycling Organisation) funded the project to plant 85,000 fruit trees in local community nurseries in Malawi. They planted one tree for every tonne of cans collected.

5 top tips for metal recyclers:

1 Wash and squash cans.

2 Push lids inside cans.

3 Use a magnet to sort steel cans.

4 Use the 'scrunch' test for crisp and chocolate wrappers.

5 Look for the recycling loop on cans.

Collage pen holder

You will need:

A clean, empty can
Construction paper
Used magazines

Glue
Scissors

Step 1
Glue a piece of construction paper around the can, leaving enough for a small overlap. Ask an adult to help you stick down the edges, as the can may be sharp.

Step 2
Cut out pictures from the magazines – try following a theme, such as football, celebrities or animals. Carefully glue the pictures on to the can.

Step 3
Fill the can up with your favourite colouring pens and pencils.

Glossary

Acids   Sour substances that can act chemically on materials to wear them away.

Aerosols   Spray cans.

Alloy   A mix of two or more metals.

Bales   Large bundles of material.

Bauxite   A kind of rock.

Carbon   A chemical element found in coal, oil, limestone and living things.

Carbon gases   Gases from industry and cars that are believed to cause climate change.

Casting   Making a metal object from a mould.

Climate change   A gradual change in the world's climate.

De-coating   Removing outer coats or layers.

Energy   Power or heat.

Feed conveyor   A conveyor belt.

Ferrous   Containing iron.

Furnaces   Large burners used to heat or melt materials.

Ingot   A slab of metal.

Iron   A heavy grey metal found in the Earth's crust.

Lacquer   A clear, protective coat.

Landfill sites   Places where rubbish is buried under the ground.

Magnet   An object that is able to pull things containing iron towards it.

Magnetic field   The force around a magnet that pulls things containing iron towards it.

Materials   Substances that other things are made out of.

Mined   Extracted from the ground.

Molten   When something solid melts and becomes liquid.

Moulds   Containers that shape materials as the materials harden.

Ores   Rocks or minerals from which materials, such as metals, can be extracted.

Oxygen   A gas found in air which has no colour or smell.

Pallets   Platforms where goods can be stacked and transported.

Precious   Very valuable.

Raw materials   Natural materials, such as rocks, wood and water.

Recycle   To use something, such as a material, again.

Rot   Break down.

Steel   A strong, durable metal that is made from a mix of iron and carbon.

Further information

Books

Metal – Re-using and Recycling Ruth Thomson,
Franklin Watts 2009

Metal – Reduce, Re-use, Recycle Alexandra Fix,
Heinemann 2007

Websites

www.canmakers.co.uk
Lots of facts on the history of cans and how they are made.

www.recycle-more.co.uk
Information on all kinds of recycling, with sections on steel
and aluminium.

www.scrib.org.uk
A website all about recycling steel cans, with a video to watch
and quiz and games sections.

Note to parents and teachers: Every effort has been made by the Publishers to
ensure that the websites in this book are suitable for children, that they are of
the highest educational value, and that they contain no inappropriate or
offensive material. However, because of the nature of the Internet, it is
impossible to guarantee that the contents of these sites will not be altered. We
strongly advise that Internet access is supervised by a responsible adult.

Index